God's Power to Help Hurting People

Student Workbook

EDITOR
COLLEEN BIRCHETT, Ph.D.

WRITER
CRYSTAL MCDOWELL

*The African American Christian
Publishing and Communications Company*
1-800-860-8642
www.urbanministries.com

First Edition
First Printing
ISBN: 0-940955-85-7

Copyright ©2003 Urban Ministries, Inc. All Rights Reserved. No part of this publication may be reproduced, stored in a retrieval system, or transmitted in any form or by any means--electronic, mechanical, photocopy, recording or otherwise--except for brief quotations in printed reviews without prior written permission from the holder of the copyright. Printed in the United States of America.

Scripture quotations are from the King James Version of the Bible unless otherwise noted.

TABLE OF CONTENTS

PREFACE 1

God's Power to Help:

1. Guilt   Rev. Zenobia Brooks 5

2. Insecurity   Dr. Dwight Perry 11

3. Low Self-Esteem   Dr. LeRoy Yates 17

4. Grief   Rev. William Butler 23

5. Powerlessness   Rev. Pellam Love 29

6. Anxiety   Dr. Loretta Reid 35

7. Fear   Bertha Swindall 41

8. Abandonment   Patricia Beason 47

9. Frustration   Rev. Paul Sadler 52

10. Depression   Dr. Pauline Reeder 58

11. Anger   Delores Holmes 63

12. Loneliness   Beverly Yates 69

PREFACE

God's Power to Help Hurting People Student Workbook

This student workbook is to be used in conjunction with the book, *God's Power to Help Hurting People*, edited by Colleen Birchett, Ph.D. It is designed to help the reader apply principles learned in the book to real-life situations. The workbook can be used in a variety of Christian Education settings, including weekday Bible studies, retreats, Vacation Bible School courses, and Christian Education Congresses. It can also be used for individual, family, or church counseling situations.

The chapters begin with a case study that contains a crisis to which a person is reacting. Each case highlights a different emotional crisis that requires intervention. After each case study there are a series of questions that allow the reader to explore how passages from the Bible apply to the problem.

The Ministry Application exercise allows the participant to either create or develop a related church-based ministry. The forms provided for each related ministry can be transferred to overhead transparencies to facilitate group participation.

The Personal Application exercises encourage each participant to take an inward look at their own struggles within each topic being considered. These questions can be used as take home assignments as well as in daily devotions.

CHAPTER ONE

CASE STUDY ON GUILT

INSTRUCTIONS: The following exercises allow you to apply principles presented in this chapter to a case study involving Tanisha, a person who feels guilty. The Bible Application exercises consist of five "discovery" questions (a-e), followed by a summary question (f). The Ministry Application section provides an opportunity for participants to incorporate some of these precepts in their local church. The Personal Application portion encourages self-examination for each participant on the subject of guilt.

TANISHA

Late one Friday afternoon, Mrs. Jackson, a social worker at the Department of Social Services, received a call from a little girl who seemed very nervous. The little girl was from the family of one of Mrs. Jackson's clients. Tanisha told Mrs. Jackson that she was frightened. Her uncle was going to come home soon, and she was afraid he would force her to have sex with him again.

She said that she had told her grandmother, but her grandmother wasn't doing anything about it. Tanisha was one of six children. All of the children had been abandoned by their mother and left with their grandmother.

In the following weeks, Mrs. Jackson went through the appropriate procedures for removing Tanisha and her brothers and sisters from their grandmother's home. The children were all placed in foster homes. Tanisha was placed in the home of one of the ladies at Mrs. Jackson's church who kept foster children.

Mrs. Brand, the woman who took Tanisha in, informed Mrs. Jackson that Tanisha told her she was the fourth child to have been sexually abused by this uncle. The little girl was very frightened and withdrawn.

Altough Mrs. Brand realized that much damage had already been done, she encouraged Tanisha to sing in the Children's Chorus, and she proceeded to get Tanisha enrolled in the church's tutorial ministry.

Shortly afterward, the choir director informed Mrs. Brand that, at choir rehearsal, Tanisha began to cry uncontrollably. When the choir director asked her what was wrong, she told him she believed that God was going to punish her and send her to hell for her sins. The choir director tried to talk to her about salvation, but felt that Tanisha was too upset to concentrate on what he was saying. He thought that her behavior was very unusual, so he called it to her foster mother's attention.

BIBLE APPLICATION EXERCISES

1. False Guilt

Many people carry false guilt that is connected with incidents over which they had no control. Others carry false guilt connected with things for which God already forgave them when they became Christians.

a. What is the scriptural basis that would ensure a person who was sexually abused that s/he has not sinned? (Ezekiel 18:1-4, 19-24, 30-31)

_____

b. Why should a child not believe that s/he has sinned merely by being born? (Psalm 139:13-17)

_____

God's Power to Help Hurting People

c. Why should a person not continue to feel guilty about sins committed before salvation? (Jeremiah 31:34; Romans 10:8-11)

_____
_____

d. How does one break the habit of harboring guilt for sins committed after salvation? (Romans 6:1-11; 1 John 1:19)

_____
_____

e. How does a believer know that God has forgiven him or her? (1 John 1:10; 2:13-16, 19)

_____
_____

f. How can a counselor use the information from questions a-e to help a counselee who carries false guilt?

_____
_____

2. Calling on the Holy Spirit in Prayer

The Holy Spirit has a role in freeing people from guilt. What types of powers are manifested through God's Spirit?

a. Genesis 1:1-5; 2:7; Job 33:4; Acts 3:1-10 _____

b. Psalm 104:30-31; Isaiah 32:14-15; Acts 2:1-2, 38-41, 47 _____

c. Exodus 31:1-11; John 16:13-15 _____

d. Numbers 11:16-17; John 14:16-18 _____

e. John 3:5-6; Galatians 5:22; 2 Corinthians 3:3; 1 Corinthians 6:11 _____

f. How can a counselor use the information from questions a-e above to prepare a counselee to call out to God in prayer?

_____

3. Leaning on God's Grace

It is important for persons who feel guilty to accept the fact that Jesus Christ died so that s/he could be forgiven for their sins.

a. Does Jesus really understand the human struggle with sin? (Hebrews 4:15-16; 2 Corinthians 12:9)

_____
_____

CASE STUDY ON GUILT

b. What has Christ done to help people who struggle with sin? (Hebrews 6:19-20; 7:25-27; 9:27-28; John 3:16)

c. How is one saved from the bondage of sin? (Acts 16:31; Ephesians 2:8; Romans 10:9; 1 John 4:15)

d. Can a person earn God's forgiveness? (Ephesians 2:5, 8)

e. What does the phrase "grace of God" mean? (1 Corinthians 1:3-7; 15:9-10; Acts 11:21-23)

f. How can the counselor use the information from questions a-e to help a counselee lean on the grace of God for forgiveness from sin?

4. FORGIVING

Forgiveness among believers plays an important part in the healing ministry of the community of faith.

a. Can a Christian really experience the love of God as long as s/he harbors resentment and hate against another person? (1 John 4:20)

b. Is it important to "forgive and forget"? (Luke 17:3)

c. Is there a relationship between forgiving and being forgiven? (Luke 6:37-38; Mark 11:25-26)

d. Why should a person be enthusiastic about forgiving others? (Matthew 18:21-35)

e. Are people who struggle with sin "out of place" in the House of the Lord? (John 8:1-11; Romans 3:23)

f. How can the information from questions a-e above be used to prepare those who want to serve in a local church's prison ministry?

5. THE ROLE OF FAITH IN HEALING

People can be healed of emotional problems, if they exercise faith in God. Explain the scriptural foundation for having faith in Jesus' power to heal emotional problems.

a. Mark 1:23-26; 5:1-13; Luke 4:33-35; Matthew 8:28-32

b. Acts 8:6-8; 16:16-18

c. Who exercised the faith that resulted in some of the demon-possessed men in Galilee being healed? What does this suggest about the role that faith plays in the counseling process? (Matthew 9:32-33; 12:22; Luke 11:14)

d. What is the relationship between faith and healing? (2 Chronicles 7:14; Hebrews 11:1-3)

e. Describe the Lord as healer. (Hosea 11:1-11; Psalm 23)

f. How can a counselor use the information from questions a-e to help a counselee understand the role of faith in healing?

6. MINISTRY APPLICATION

Outline a plan to create or improve one of the following:
a) a partnership with a local crisis center that assists victims of sexual abuse
b) a prison ministry

Focus Scripture:_____

Objectives:
a._____
b._____

How can your ministry incorporate the following?
1. Biblically-based counseling

a._____
b._____

2. Non-counseling services

a._____
b._____

3. What parts of the program would cost money?

a._____
b._____

4. Where would you get the funds?

a._____
b._____

How can other ministries educate people about the difference between real and false guilt?
a. Church School?

_____

b. Weekly Bible study classes? _____

c. Other? _____

_____

7. PERSONAL APPLICATION

What are your general reactions to the devotional at the beginning of Chapter 1?
_____
_____
_____

Describe sources of feelings of guilt in your life.
_____
_____
_____
_____

Are you doing things that you know are wrong? (1 John 1:9)
_____
_____
_____

Who is the author of false guilt? (Revelations 12:10-11)
_____
_____
_____

How can you be free from the yoke of guilt? (Galatians 5:1)
_____
_____
_____

What does Romans 8:1 mean to you?
_____
_____
_____

Begin to resist any thoughts of condemnation by praying Romans 8:1 to yourself on a daily basis.

CHAPTER TWO

CASE STUDY ON INSECURITY

INSTRUCTIONS: The following exercises will lead to an in-depth study of John's problem of insecurity based on the principles that were introduced in this chapter. The Bible Application exercises consist of five "discovery" questions (a-e), followed by a summary question (f). The Ministry Application section provides an opportunity for participants to apply some of these precepts in their local church. The Personal Application portion encourages self-exploration for each participant regarding insecurity.

JOHN

When John entered his brother Paul's home, it seemed that all of the sadness of the months before came over him at once. His voice broke, and tears entered his eyes as he sat on the couch across from his brother and began to talk. By now, his family had heard the news. John had been dismissed from his position as pastor because he had falsified information on his employment application. He had told the congregation that he graduated from seminary, but he hadn't. A member found out from a former classmate and took the matter to the church authorities, after spreading rumors related to it all over the church. The church authorities verified the story and then asked John to leave his position.

John told Paul that seminary had been very difficult for him and he had been asked to leave in his final year, because he failed all of his classes. He was informed of his dismissal from the school just before graduation exercises. He had lied to his parents in order to prevent them from coming to the graduation exercises and not seeing him there. He never told the church he hadn't graduated, rationalizing that he had finished four years of seminary, which was really the requirement for the job.

As John talked, his brother recalled earlier times when both he and John had been pressured by their father to enter the ministry. Their father was an ordained minister. Paul remembered how he had dropped out of seminary, deciding that the ministry was not his calling. He remembered how devastated his parents had been, and how John, his younger brother, had entered the seminary, hoping not to disappoint his parents as Paul apparently had done.

As John talked, Paul said a quiet prayer, hoping he would be able to help John through the traumatic experience he was describing.

BIBLE APPLICATION EXERCISES

1. THE BENEFITS OF FAILURE

Insecure people such as John can be overwhelmed by what appears to be a failure on their part. However Christians can see failure in a different light.

a. Will God fail His own people? (Deuteronomy 31:6)_____

b. What does it mean when life does not turn out the way a person expects? If something doesn't turn out right, what does that mean? (Romans 8:28)_____

c. Perceived failure is really adversity. What are some outcomes of adversity for the person who loves the Lord? (Genesis 30:27; Romans 5:4; Hebrews 5:8)_____

d. What can a child of God expect to happen during a time of adversity? (Isaiah 30:19-21)

e. What attitude should a child of God have about adversity? (Job 1:20-22)

f. In what ways could a counselor use the answers to a-e to help a person such as John accept the fact that s/he may not do well in a particular college or career?

2. God's Love

The way of the world computes personal worth in terms of whether one can meet expectations of parents and others. However, God's love is the only real basis for a Christian's acceptance of self.

a. How is God different from the authority figures at the workplace? (1 Corinthians 13:8-13)

b. What is the relationship between one's personal "deficiencies" and God's love? (Proverbs 10:12)

c. Why is it more important for a Christian to cultivate loving relationships with family and church, rather than pursuing godless liaisons at work for the sake of promotions? (Proverbs 15:17)

d. In what ways does God's love help people become the best persons that they can be? (Jeremiah 31:3)

e. What role does the church play in helping people experience God's love? (1 John 4:7-12)

f. How can the answers to a-e above be used to help an insecure person cope with lack of acceptance from others? How can these Scriptures be used to help a person deal with a demanding, rejecting parent?

CASE STUDY ON INSECURITY

3. God's Opinion of Human Beings

Insecure people are often in bondage to others' opinions and thoughts. In contrast, what is God's opinion about human beings as reflected in His Word?

a. Genesis 1:31 _____

b. Psalm 139:13-18 _____

c. John 3:16 _____

d. In whose image have all human beings been created? (Genesis 1:27) _____

e. How does God see those who believe in Him? (Exodus 19:6; 1 Peter 2:5, 9)
_____
_____

f. Using the answers to a-e, how does God's opinion of a person contrast with those held by racists and others who judge people by outward appearances?
_____
_____

4. The Importance of Wise Counsel

Some insecure people try to fight insecurity through academic accomplishments, high salaried positions, memberships in prestigious clubs, and keeping company with people perceived as high achievers. However, the Bible says that one of the best ways to fight insecurity is with wise counsel from God and from godly people.

a. In what ways does the Lord help a Christian deal with oppression on his/her job? What role does wise counsel play? (Psalm 73:21-26) _____

b. What are some reasons a Christian should pursue godly counsel instead of privately dealing with thoughts that result from oppression and adversity? (Proverbs 11:14)
_____
_____

c. How will the Lord judge people? What role will wise counsel have? (Isaiah 11:1-4)
_____
_____

d. What role does the Holy Spirit have in providing wise counsel? (John 14:15-21; 15:26)
_____
_____

e. How can the church provide an environment where people can become confident? (Psalm 108:35-43)

f. Considering the answers to a-e, what role does prayer, Scripture study, and fellowship with believers have in discouraging insecure feelings?

5. Attacking Satan's Lies

Satan has a special package of lies for insecure people. In order for an insecure person to maintain a positive attitude, the person will have to attack Satan's lies with the Word of God. Refute the following lies of Satan using the Scriptures suggested plus any other Scriptures that apply.

a. Lie #1: A person should be "sized up" based on outward appearances such as: job, expensive clothing, skin color, place of residence, family connections, or educational achievement. (Isaiah 28:29; 30:1)

b. Lie #2: Only "high class" people (in the world's terms) should hold positions of leadership (such as deacon) in the church. (Romans 12:2; 1 Corinthians 11:18; Revelations 20:11-12)

c. Lie #3: It is important for a man to be number one in everything he does. (2 Corinthians 10:12; 1 Corinthians 12)

d. Lie #4: A real woman or man is one who can control others at all times, particularly his/her spouse. (1 Peter 5:1-7; Proverbs 15:33; Ephesians 5:21-33)

e. Lie #5: Corporate America is seen by many as the center of the universe-where the action is. (James 1:17; Hebrews 12:9; Matthew 28:18)

f. How can each of the above lies play a part in causing a person to become insecure about who the person is? How can a counselor use this exercise to help an insecure person?

CASE STUDY ON INSECURITY

6. MINISTRY APPLICATION

Create a plan for a support group for people experiencing insecurity on the job.

Focus Scripture: _____

Objectives:
a. _____
b. _____

1. What are some topics or themes? _____

2. What type of guest speakers should be invited?

   a. _____
   b. _____
   c. _____

3. What biblical coping skills would be taught?

   a. _____
   b. _____
   c. _____

4. What are some skills related to dealing with discrimination/harassment that can be taught?

   a. _____
   b. _____
   c. _____

5. Describe some exercises or activities that can help an insecure person to see him/herself differently.

_____
_____
_____

7. PERSONAL APPLICATION

What are your general reactions to the devotional at the beginning of Chapter 2?
_____
_____
_____

What makes you feel insecure sometimes?
_____
_____
_____

How can you become more secure? (Matthew 17:20)
_____
_____
_____

When do you feel separated from the love of God? (Romans 8:38-39)
_____
_____
_____

Describe a time when you really felt that you trusted in Christ.
_____
_____
_____

Which Scripture used within this chapter matches most closely with your life? Why?
_____
_____
_____

CHAPTER THREE

CASE STUDY ON LOW SELF-ESTEEM

INSTRUCTIONS: In the following story, James is experiencing low self-esteem that is in part due to reactions against racism that he has encountered in society.

The following exercises lead to an in-depth study of James' problem, and provide the opportunity to apply principles covered in this chapter to helping people with similar problems. The Bible Application exercises consist of five "discovery" questions (a-e), followed by a summary question (f). The Ministry Application section requires summarizing and applying information gained from the first five exercises. The Personal Application section provides an opportunity for self-examination and reflection.

JAMES

Late one Saturday afternoon, Brother Fraser, the newly appointed youth pastor, was preparing his Sunday School lesson, when his telephone rang. It was Mrs. Young, the mother of Neesha, one of the students in his class.

Mrs. Young was in tears. James, her 20-year-old son, had fallen 14 stories to the ground outside of the building where he was working as a window washer. He had been in a coma for several days and today had awakened for the first time. Mrs. Young openly thanked God that, while James was cut and bruised and had some internal injuries, he had no broken bones, was not paralyzed, and was not brain damaged.

Mrs. Young asked Brother Fraser if he would visit her son in the hospital. Brother Fraser agreed and visited him several times. It was during these weekly visits that James opened up to Brother Fraser. He told him he had a damaged past that only recently he had begun trying to repair.

He said that, by the time he was 13 years old, he had stopped attending church with his mother and sister and had dropped out of school. This led to arguments with his mother, so he left home and started living on the streets. He joined a gang near the housing projects where his family lived and dropped out of the trade school he had been attending.

He said that he dropped out of school because of racism. He had once been very excited about the courses he was taking in electrical wiring, but he noticed some of the White male teachers did not like answering his questions. They paid much more attention to the White male students and seemed to ignore James.

The "straw that broke the camel's back" happened when James attempted, through the school, to find a part-time summer job working with an electrical wiring company. He was ignored by the employers who recruited for part-time help at the school. Instead, he was offered a job washing windows, at a rate that was much lower than the money being paid to White students.

James became angry and quit both school and church, believing that, if God loved Black people, He would not allow racism to exist. Before long, he began snorting cocaine. He had nearly overdosed several times. Soon he began to rob homes, stores, and other places to get the money he needed for cocaine. This is what started his brushes with "the law."

He had been in and out of juvenile homes and jails throughout his teenaged years. He deeply resented some of the White people who ran these places and the White police officers who, once he had a record, regularly harassed him on the streets. He was currently on probation and had promised the probation officer that he would accept a part-time job washing windows to pay room and board at his mother's home, as a condition of being released on probation. It hadn't been a month since he had been making a new start that the accident took place.

Over and over again, James said he had been held back by racism. While he acknowledged there were many African American men who had been successful in spite of racism, Brother Fraser could see that James did not feel he was one who could make it, against the odds.

BIBLE APPLICATION EXERCISES

1. A Relationship with God

James left the church because he felt that God favored White people over Blacks.

a. Are Black people excluded from God's plan of salvation? (John 3:16; Acts 10:34; Psalm 139:12; James 2:1-5)_____

b. Does Jesus know how it feels to be discriminated against? (John 1:46)_____

c. What was the likely complexion of Jews in biblical times? (Genesis 15:13; Genesis 9)
_____

d. In whose image is James made? (Genesis 1:26)_____

e. What does God promise James? (Isaiah 26:3; Luke 2:14)_____

f. How would you use the information from questions a-e to lead an African American with low self-esteem (as a result of discrimination they have experienced) to Christ?
_____

2. Self-Reflection

To develop self-esteem, James must be open to developing an opinion of himself that is separate from the opinions held by others.

a. Study James' life again, in the previous story. What are some of the talents and abilities that God has given to him? (1 Corinthians 12)
_____

b. What potential does James have? (1 Peter 2:5, 9)_____

c. Once James accepts Jesus Christ as his Saviour, who is he? How is this the basis of a new self-image? (2 Corinthians 5:17; James 1:9-11)_____
_____

d. What are some characteristics that come along with salvation? How can these become a part of James' new self-image? (2 Corinthians 12)_____
_____

e. What evidence is there, in Scripture, that "God didn't make junk"? (Genesis 1:27)
_____

CASE STUDY ON LOW SELF-ESTEEM

f. How could a counselor use the information from questions a-e to guide James into meaningful and productive self-reflection?

3. AN AFFIRMATIVE ACTION PLAN
James needs to develop an affirmative action plan for himself, based on the Word of God.

a. What is the biblical basis for this plan? (Romans 12:2)

b. What is the biblical basis for setting goals? (Genesis 1:1-5)

c. Once James accepts Christ, does he have what it takes to achieve his goals? (Psalm 23; Acts 1:8)

d. How should James go about preparing for a career? (2 Timothy 2:15)

e. What should James do about his old friends? (2 Corinthians 6:17)

f. How could a counselor use the information from questions a-e in helping James to set new goals for his life?

4. DEALING WITH ADVERSITY
James can be shown that adversity is a blessing in disguise.

a. What is one basic fact about adversity? (Romans 8:28)

b. From the life of David, what do we learn about adversity? (1 Samuel 17:37, 45, 47, 50, 54)

c. Does dealing with adversity involve fighting with human beings? (Ephesians 6:10-18)

d. What will be the outcome of adversity for the Christian? (James 1:12)

e. What is the source of power to overcome adversity? (Matthew 28:18; Acts 1:8)

f. How can a person use the information from questions a-e above to demonstrate to James that some of the things that happened to him are blessings in disguise?

5. Mrs. Young

It is usually very difficult for a single woman to raise a young African American man who has low self-esteem. However, the Bible does contain guidelines, promises, and models for Christian women who are in this situation.

a. Does God care about the problems encountered by women raising sons alone? (Luke 7:11-15; Hebrews 11:35) _____
_____
_____

b. What promise can Mrs. Young claim from the Lord, based on Isaiah 66:6-14?
_____
_____
_____

c. What does 1 Corinthians 3:1, 2 and 1 Thessalonians 2:7 suggest about Mrs. Young's approach to James? _____
_____
_____

d. How can a woman such as Mrs. Young use Psalm 139:13-19 to help her son develop a healthy self-image? _____
_____
_____

e. Was Ephesians 6:9 intended for men only? What applications are there for single-parent women?
_____
_____
_____

f. Thousands of Black women are attempting to raise Black sons whose self-images have been damaged, due to effects of racism. What specific guidelines can be developed from the previous Scriptures, and applied in this difficult situation?
_____
_____
_____

6. MINISTRY APPLICATION

Create an employment ministry based in a local church.

Focus Scripture: _____

Objectives:
a. _____

b. _____

1. What services would be provided?
_____
_____

2. How would the employment ministry help people to discover their gifts and talents?

a. _____

b. _____

c. _____

3. How would the ministry help people to use their gifts and talents to locate jobs?

a. _____

b. _____

c. _____

4. How would the ministry help to build self-esteem?
_____
_____

7. PERSONAL APPLICATION

When do you struggle with low self-esteem?
_____
_____
_____

What gifts has God given you? (1 Corinthians 12:7)
_____
_____
_____

What talents do you have?
_____
_____
_____

What strengths do other people see in you?
_____
_____
_____

What are some organizations in your church where your gifts and talents can contribute to the building of God's kingdom?
_____
_____
_____

CHAPTER FOUR

CASE STUDY ON GRIEF

INSTRUCTIONS: The following exercises require applying principles presented in this chapter to a case study involving Brandy, a person who is hurting from grief. The Bible Application exercises consist of five "discovery" questions (a-e), followed by a summary question (f). The Ministry Application section provides an opportunity for participants to incorporate some of these precepts in their local churches. The Personal Application portion encourages self-examination regarding the subject of grief.

BRANDY

It was Christmas time, and Mrs. Blackwell, Superintendent of the Church School, was making her usual rounds to see if all of the teachers had arrived. When she got to the class for teenagers, she noticed that Brandy, the teaching assistant, was absent again. This disturbed Mrs. Blackwell, because Brandy had been showing signs of emotional stress lately, and had missed quite a few Sundays with the students. She hadn't been to the teacher's meetings, either.

After church, Mrs. Blackwell decided to pay Brandy a surprise visit. Brandy was happy to see her and invited her in. During the conversation that followed, Brandy broke down in tears. She told Mrs. Blackwell that she was suffering from a hangover. She had been out drinking the night before and felt too sick to teach her class. She said that she didn't want to be this way, but that she couldn't help herself

She said that she, her brother, and some friends had been going out to lounges lately, drinking heavily. She had also used amphetamines and had smoked some marijuana. This had been going on, off and on, since she was a teenager. She was now 27 years old.

She had made a commitment to Christ, and, for the past year, had stopped drinking and smoking marijuana. However, during the holidays she felt weaker than ever and couldn't prevent herself from yielding to the old desires for drugs. She was disappointed that she could no longer be a role model for her Church School students. She felt that she had failed in her attempt to be a Christian.

She told Mrs. Blackwell about her search for a relationship with a man and how frustrated she was that most of her relationships ended up being "one night stands." She also told Mrs. Blackwell about her painful childhood. Her mother and father had both become alcoholics, and were unable to take care of her and her brother. The courts had taken them away from her parents when she was 12 years old, and since then, they had been moved from one foster home to another until they had reached the age of 18.

At the end of the conversation, Brandy admitted that she needed help but didn't know where to turn.

BIBLE APPLICATION EXERCISES

1. RELATIONSHIP LOSS

Brandy suffered from the loss of the relationship between herself and her natural family. It appears that she never attended to the grief she experienced, and is still searching for the nurturing relationship she lost.

Describe the relational losses of the following people from the Bible:

a. Mary Magdalene, Joanna, and Mary, the mother of James, after they discovered the empty tomb (Luke 24:1-12, John 20:1-20) _____

God's Power to Help Hurting People

b. Peter during the crucifixion and after discovering the empty tomb (Luke 22:45-62, John 20:1-20)
___

c. In the Old Testament Hagar suffered a similar loss when she was ostracized from the family of Sarah and Abraham. Who was Hagar? (Genesis 21:9-10)
___

d. What was the relationship between Hagar and the family of Sarah and Abraham? (Genesis 16:1)
___

e. Describe Hagar's relational loss. (Genesis 21:1-18) ___
___

f. How did the experiences of Hagar, Mary Magdalene, Joanna, Mary the mother of James, and Peter also reflect psychological, authority/responsibility, systemic, and functional losses?
___

2. Functional Loss

Alcoholism and drug dependency have eroded Brandy's ability to function as she once did as a Church School teacher. She also appears to be grieving the loss of her independence from drug use.

a. In the Old Testament Samson suffered a functional loss. Who was Samson? (Judges 13:2-5, 24)
___

b. What was Samson's relationship with the Philistines? (Judges 14:1-20) ___

c. Describe Samson's functional loss. (Judges 16) ___
___

d. Describe the Apostle Paul's functional loss on the road to Damascus. (Acts 9:3-9)
___

e. What was the outcome of Paul's loss experience? (Acts 9:20-29) ___
___

f. In what ways are the stories of Samson and the Apostle Paul also examples of systemic and functional losses? ___
___

3. Psychological Loss

Brandy's decision for Christ provided a new image of someone who was loved by Christ and worthy to be loved. She didn't need the false support of controlled substances. Her compassion for her students caused them to see her as a good role model. However, her return to drinking caused her to suffer the loss of this image and replace it with a negative one.

a. Elijah suffered a similar loss of image as he fled from Jezebel. What was Elijah's image of himself before his flight from Jezebel? (1 Kings 17) What was Elijah's image before the people? (1 Kings 18)
___

CASE STUDY ON GRIEF

b. What was the threat that Elijah faced from Jezebel? (1 Kings 19) _____

c. Describe Elijah's image of himself as he fled from Jezebel. (1 Kings 19:1-4) _____

d. The Apostle Peter also suffered a psychological loss. What image did Peter have of himself prior to his denial of Christ? (Matthew 16:21-22; 17:1-5)

e. What type of image loss did Peter experience after his denial of Christ? (Mark 14:66-72; Luke 22:55-62; John 18:15-18, 25-27)

f. To what extent are the stories of Elijah and Peter also examples of the threat of functional or role/responsibility losses?

4. Authority/Role/Responsibility Loss

As a Church School teacher, Brandy had a certain amount of authority and responsibility. Because she is no longer teaching, Brandy is experiencing loss in this area and is grieving from it.

a. In the Old Testament, Saul suffered from a loss of authority, role, and responsibility in Israel. What was Saul's original role in Israel? (1 Samuel 11; 12; 17:1-2; 19:1-2; 13:1)

b. What caused Saul to lose his position in Israel? (1 Samuel 13:13-14) _____

c. Describe Saul's unattended grief and the behaviors that followed. (1 Samuel 16:19-23; 18:10-11, 17-18; 19:9-11) _____

d. Describe the disciples' functional loss upon the death, burial, resurrection, and ascension of Jesus Christ. (Luke 15:11-32) _____

e. How did the Great Commission help the disciples cope with their grief? (Matthew 28:18-20)

f. In what sense are the losses of Saul and the disciples also examples of relationship and systemic losses?

5. Systemic and Material Losses

Since they rarely stayed in one foster home, Brandy and her brother were separated from one family system after another. They experienced a loss of each family system. They also experienced material losses such as furniture and bedrooms that they had to leave behind.

a. Ruth, Naomi, and Orpah also suffered from systemic and material losses. What were Naomi's systemic losses? (Ruth 1:1, 3, 5-6) _____
_____

b. Compare Ruth and Orpah's systemic losses with those of Naomi. (Ruth 1:8-22)_____
_____

c. In what ways were the losses of Ruth, Naomi, and Orpah also material losses? (Ruth 1:8-22)
_____

d. Describe Zacchaeus' systemic loss when he decided to climb down from the tree and meet Jesus. (Luke 19:1-10) _____
_____

e. In what way was Zacchaeus' loss also a material one? (Luke 19:8-10)_____
_____
_____

f. In what sense are the losses of Ruth, Naomi, Orpah, and Zacchaeus also relational and functional losses?
_____
_____

6. MINISTRY APPLICATION

Develop a Church School elective of 13 weeks on the topic of grieving.

Focus Scripture: _____

Objectives:
a._____

b._____

1. Where would Church School teachers get training on the subject of grief?

a._____

b._____

2. What types of literature or videos should be offered as supplemental material?

a._____

b._____

3. How could the Church School provide support to people grieving from:

a. Relational losses_____

b. Psychological losses_____

c. Systematic losses _____

d. Material losses _____

e. Functional losses _____

4. What are other topics that would be covered?
_____
_____
_____

7. PERSONAL APPLICATION

What types of losses have you experienced?
_____
_____
_____

What does the Bible say about your pain? (Hebrews 4:15)
_____
_____
_____

What hope is there concerning your pain? (Psalms 30:5; Ecclesiastes 3:4)
_____
_____
_____

How can you cope? (Romans 8:26)
_____
_____
_____

What friends can support you as you journey through this process?
_____
_____
_____

CHAPTER FIVE

CASE STUDY ON POWERLESSNESS

INSTRUCTIONS: In the following story, Drake is a person who feels powerless. The following exercises lead into an in-depth study of Drake's problem, based on the principles that were introduced in this chapter.

The Bible Application exercises consist of five "discovery" questions (a-e), followed by a summary question (f). The Ministry Application section provides an opportunity to incorporate some of these precepts in local churches. The Personal Application section encourages self-examination on the subject of powerlessness.

DRAKE

Drake, a veteran of the Marine Corps who once served in Vietnam, made an appointment with the counseling ministry at his church. During the session, he informed Brother Wilson that he had recently been laid off from his job at the plant. He had three small children. He was visibly upset because his marriage was unstable. He described how he and his wife had separated and then reunited, off and on, in cycles over the past few years, due to his drinking problem.

He was currently trying to earn a G.E.D. (General Educational Diploma), but he was distracted by his problems at home. He was receiving veterans' educational benefits but was afraid that he might lose them because his grades were bad and his attendance was irregular.

What was of immediate concern to Drake was a situation that had arisen at the company from which he had been laid off. The company had offered to give him a large sum of money to purchase the seniority that he had accumulated over the past 10 years at the automobile factory. Drake felt a sense of powerlessness in relationship to the big company. He felt pressured to take the money, even though he knew that it was not enough to pay for tools, uniforms, and other expenses that he would have.

Another problem that Drake discussed with the counselor was his relationship with his mother. His mother would, regardless of his successes or failures, always compare him with his older brother and say that he did not measure up. She also manipulated him, insisting that he should be loyal to her, regardless of whether she was right or wrong. Drake felt powerless in relationship to his mother, and he felt manipulated by her.

BIBLE APPLICATION EXERCISES

1. DRAKE'S MARRIAGE

a. How does knowing Matthew 28:18 positively influence Drake as he deals with his marital problems?
_____

b. How can understanding John 19:11 help Drake understand power struggles in marriage?
_____

c. What might be some of Drake's unmet needs in his marriage? How can God meet these needs?
_____

d. What might be some of his wife's unmet needs in her marriage? How can God meet these needs?
_____

e. What are the riches that God offers to Drake as he tries to improve his marriage? (1 Corinthians 12; Galatians 5:22) _____
_____

f. What are some of the goals that Drake can set for his marriage? How can the information in exercises a-e be used to help remove the sense of powerlessness in Drake's marriage? How can church leaders use this information to improve African American marriages at various stages of the life cycle?
_____
_____

2. Drake's Mother

a. How does knowing Matthew 28:18 positively influence Drake as he relates to his mother?
_____
_____
_____

b. How can understanding John 19:11 help Drake understand power struggles involving parents?
_____
_____
_____

c. What might be some of Drake's unmet needs in relationship to his mother? How can God meet these needs? _____
_____

d. What might be some of his mother's unmet needs? How can God meet these needs?
_____

e. What are some of the riches that God offers to Drake as he tries to improve his relationship with his mother? (1 Corinthians 12; Galatians 5:22) _____
_____

f. What types of goals can Drake set for his relationship with his mother? How can the information in exercises a-e be used to remove the sense of powerlessness in his relationship to his mother? How can this information be used to improve other relationships between married adults and seemingly overbearing parents?
_____
_____

3. Drake's Job/Career

a. How can understanding Matthew 28:18 influence Drake's approach to career planning?
_____
_____

CASE STUDY ON POWERLESSNESS

b. What is the scriptural evidence that shows God's support of Drake during his career development? (Job 1:18; Romans 8:31) _____

c. What is one step that Drake should take in order to remain positive about seeking employment? (Ephesians 4:29) What are possible sources of negative thinking that Drake should avoid? (Philippians 4:8) _____

d. Does Drake have reason to worry? (Job 1:10) Why or why not? _____

e. What changes in behavior are necessary for Drake to obtain meaningful and secure employment? _____

f. Using the information from exercises a-e, what are some ways that a counselor can help Drake to remove a sense of powerlessness as he plans a career? What are some ways that this information can help counselors minister more effectively to other African American men who are unemployed and feeling powerless? _____

4. Drake's Company

a. List the ways that Drake can approach those who want him to sell his seniority. (Matthew 28:18) _____

b. How can understanding John 19:11 help Drake deal with power struggles with the company? _____

c. What might be some of Drake's unmet needs in relationship to the company? How can God meet these needs? _____

d. What might be some of the company's unmet needs in relationship to Drake? How can God meet these needs? _____

e. What are some of the riches that God offers to Drake as he negotiates with his company? (1 Corinthians 12; Galatians 5:22) _____

f. What types of goals can Drake set for his relationship with the company? How can the information in exercises a-e be used to remove the sense of powerlessness in his relationship with the big company? How can counselors use this information to help people cope when their companies lay them off or relocate? _____
_____

5. Drake's Problem with Alcohol

a. List the ways that Drake can approach his problem with alcohol. (Matthew 28:18)
_____
_____
_____

b. How could understanding John 19:11 help Drake with his power struggles with alcohol?
_____
_____
_____

c. What might be some of Drake's unmet needs that alcohol seems to fulfill? How can God meet these needs? _____
_____
_____

d. How can Drake's problem with alcohol be broken down into parts? What types of goals should he set? _____
_____

e. What are the riches that God offers Drake as his dependency on alcohol is reduced? (2 Corinthians 12:9; Philippians 4:13) _____
_____

f. How can Drake use the information from exercises a-e to set goals for overcoming his dependency on alcohol? How can counselors use the information from exercises a-e to help those who escape through drugs and alcohol in response to being unemployed?
_____
_____

CASE STUDY ON POWERLESSNESS

6. MINISTRY APPLICATION

Develop an intervention team to help members who struggle with substance abuse and feelings of powerlessness.

Focus Scripture: _____

Objectives:
a. _____

b. _____

1. What training will be necessary for the intervention team?

a. _____

b. _____

2. What type of people would make the best team members?

a. _____

b. _____

c. _____

3. What kind of commitment is necessary for the team members?

a. _____

b. _____

c. _____

4. How could an intervention team help Drake complete the following planning form?

PROBLEM	GOAL	DEADLINE
_____	_____	_____
_____	_____	_____
_____	_____	_____
_____	_____	_____
_____	_____	_____

7. PERSONAL APPLICATION

What situations cause you to feel powerless?
_____
_____

What is the primary source of your sense of powerlessness in these situations?
_____
_____

Is there any hope? What hope is there?
_____
_____

What role does the Holy Spirit play? (2 Corinthians 12:9-10)
_____
_____

Select a set of seven Scriptures from this chapter for reflection and memorization.
_____
_____

CHAPTER SIX

CASE STUDY ON ANXIETY

INSTRUCTIONS: In the following story, Mrs. Ellis is experiencing anxiety. The following exercises will lead to an in-depth study of Mrs. Ellis' problem, based on the principles that were introduced in this chapter.

The Bible Application exercises consist of five "discovery" questions (a-e), followed by a summary question (f). The Ministry Application section provides an opportunity for participants to incorporate some of the precepts in their local churches. The Personal Application portion encourages self-examination on the subject of anxiety.

MOTHER ELLIS

Deacon Jemison, as usual, was administering communion to the sick and shut-in of Olivet Baptist Church. It was the first Sunday morning. When he got to Mother Ellis' home, he noticed something was wrong. Although it was 10:30 a.m., she had the venetian blinds closed throughout the house. She invited him in and sat in her rocking chair, with a blanket covering her feet.

She told Deacon Jemison she was afraid that someone would break in. She also said she was convinced that she had a serious heart condition, even though the doctors said they didn't find a problem. She said she was experiencing difficulty in breathing and her chest felt heavy.

During the following weeks, Deacon Jemison continued to visit Mother Ellis on his usual sick visitation rounds. During his visits, he got to know Mother Ellis outside of the usual environment of the church. Mother Ellis told him that she had been forced to move in with her sister because she could no longer pay the mortgage on her home. Her husband had died last year. She had recently been forced to retire from a job she had held for twenty years, cleaning office buildings, because she had reached the age of 65. However, the job didn't provide retirement benefits.

She was finding it difficult to "make ends meet" on the combination of food stamps and Social Security benefits that she was receiving. Her relationship with her sister with whom she shared the apartment had never been harmonious, and there were a number of old family conflicts that had never been resolved. However, she had been keeping all these troubles to herself. She was worried that one day her sister and she would have an argument and she would be put out in the street. She hadn't been coming to church because she was worried that people would notice that her clothes were no longer in fashion.

BIBLE APPLICATION EXERCISES

1. GOD'S FAITHFULNESS

Deacon Jemison could remind Mother Ellis that God is faithful and will be with her in this stressful situation. How can these scriptural references help reduce Mother Ellis' anxiety? What do the Scriptures indicate about God's faithfulness?

a. Philippians 4:6, 7
_____

b. 1 Peter 5:7
_____

c. John 14:27
_____

God's Power to Help Hurting People

d. Psalm 37:25

e. For what can Mother Ellis be thankful? (Psalm 43:5) _____

f. If you were a member of the sick visitation team at your church, and were visiting Mother Ellis, how would you make use of the information from exercises a-e?

2. God's Power

Deacon Jemison could remind Mother Ellis of God's awesome power. What do the scriptural references reveal about God's power in Mother Ellis' situation?

a. Psalm 27:3 _____

b. Matthew 28:18 _____

c. Genesis 1 _____

d. Psalm 23 _____

e. What can Mother Ellis learn from the life of Abraham about the awesome power of God? How does this apply to Mother Ellis' current situation?

f. If you were on the sick visitation team, visiting Mother Ellis, how would you make use of information from exercises a-e above?

3. God in Times of Weakness

Deacon Jemison could remind Mother Ellis that God can "come through" in a time of weakness. What is the scriptural basis for God's willingness to act on the behalf of the weak? How does each passage relate to Mother Ellis' situation?

a. Matthew 6:31, 32

b. Philippians 4:19

CASE STUDY ON ANXIETY

c. Proverbs 3:26

d. Philippians 4:13

e. Corinthians 12:9

f. If you were on the sick visitation team, visiting Mother Ellis, how would you make use of the information from exercises a-e?

4. WE MUST WAIT ON GOD

Deacon Jemison could remind Mother Ellis to wait on God. How do the following Scripture references relate to Mother Ellis' situation? What does each indicate about waiting on God?

a. Isaiah 30:15

b. Job 14:14

c. Isaiah 40:31

d. Habakkuk 2:3

e. What do the lives of Abraham and Sarah show about waiting on the Lord? How does this apply to Mother Ellis' situation?

f. If you were on the sick visitation team, visiting Mother Ellis, how would you make use of information from exercises a-e above?

5. God Will Come on Time

Deacon Jemison could remind Mother Ellis that God will come in His own timing. How do the following Scripture references relate to Mother Ellis' life? What does each reveal about God's timing?

a. Proverbs 14:26
_____
_____
_____

b. Exodus 16:14-35
_____
_____
_____

c. Exodus 17:5-7
_____
_____
_____

d. Luke 11:5-10
_____
_____
_____

e. Matthew 18:12-14; Luke 15:4-7
_____
_____
_____

f. If you were on the sick visitation team, visiting Mother Ellis, how would you make use of the information from exercises a-e?
_____
_____

6. MINISTRY APPLICATION

Form a Serving Our Seniors (S.O.S.) committee.

Focus Scripture:
_____

Objectives:
a._____

b._____

How might your ministry provide for each of the following?

Need	**Plan for Providing**
Food	_____
Finances	_____
Counseling	_____
Referrals	_____
Housing	_____
Fellowship	_____
Employment (part-time)	_____

7. PERSONAL APPLICATION

What makes you anxious?
_____
_____

Have you ever felt trepidation and fear about future events? Explain.
_____
_____

What thoughts or beliefs relate to your fears?
_____
_____

Locate four Scriptures that are about fear. How can they help you?
_____
_____

What does Philippians 4:6-8 mean to you?
_____
_____

Write Philippians 4:6-8 on small pieces of notebook paper and post them around your home to remind you of God's peace.

CHAPTER SEVEN

CASE STUDY ON FEAR

INSTRUCTIONS: The following exercises below apply principles presented in this chapter to a case study involving a person who is hurting from fear. The Bible Application exercises consist of five "discovery" questions (a-e), followed by a summary question (f). The Ministry Application section provides an opportunity for participants to incorporate some of these precepts in their local church. The Personal Application portion encourages self-examination on the subject of fear.

ALICE'S MOTHER

Sixteen-year-old Alice came to the Oak Street Baptist's shelter, seeking a meal and a place to rest. She had run away from home but didn't have a job. She found life on the streets too foreign to her, and she didn't feel that she could cope any longer. She told Mrs. Carey, the woman on duty, that she wanted to return to her parents, but she felt that she needed an adult to go home with her.

The following day, Mrs. Carey and Alice left the shelter and went to Alice's home. Alice's mother seemed grateful to see her again and embraced her tearfully. However, one week later, Alice's mother came to the shelter and asked for counseling from Mrs. Carey on what to do with her daughter. She was afraid her daughter might leave again.

Alice's mother told Mrs. Carey that Alice was rebelling because she no longer wanted to obey house rules. Alice had asked many times if she could go to after-school activities at her school and church, but her mother had said she could not. Alice's mother was afraid that, if she allowed Alice to interact with other teenagers, she would sooner or later become pregnant, just as her mother had. As a single parent with very few friends, Alice's mother was very careful about who came to her home. She insisted that Alice spend her time with family members only, and that she use any extra time she had either studying or doing housework.

She was sending her to church so that she could get some Bible training from the people there. However, Alice's mother was surprised one day when Alice asked her if she could go to a basketball game with a boy from her church. This led to an argument over when Alice would be old enough to date.

Alice wanted to begin dating because she had reached her 16th birthday. However, her mother set the dating age at 21, when she felt that Alice would be accountable for all her own actions. Alice tried to explain how she felt about the boy at church, but her mother slapped her, feeling that she was being disrespectful. She was particularly angry because Alice did not fear her enough to keep her feelings to herself.

This year, when school began and it was time to buy Alice's clothes for school, Alice told her mother she wanted to select her own clothing. This led to another argument. Shortly after that incident, Alice failed to come home from school one day and hadn't been seen since.

While she was back home now, none of the original issues that led to Alice's leaving home had been resolved. Spring was coming, and Alice's mother was afraid that as soon as the weather was warm enough Alice would return to the streets again.

BIBLE APPLICATION EXERCISES

1. FACING FEAR

One of the first steps Alice's mother must take in dealing with her situation is to recognize the degree to which fear is controlling her life. What thought process could lead Alice's mother (who has a

child born out of wedlock) to be fearful about?
a. Attending church? (Matthew 21:28-32) _____
_____

b. She is afraid of not being loved by anyone other than her child? (John 8:1-12; Romans 3:23; 5:12; Ephesians 2:8) _____
_____

c. Is the child merely an extension of the parent? How might misunderstanding the role of parent and child lead to unfounded fears with the Lord and others? (Psalm 139:13-17)
_____

d. Are the parents judged for the sins of their children and vice versa? (Ezekiel 18:2-4, 19-24, 30-31)
_____

e. Is there any hope for a fearful person? (1 John 4:7-10, 15-16, 18; 2 Corinthians 12:9)
_____

f. How could a counselor use the information from questions a-e to help fearful parents?
_____

2. Recognizing "Dysfunctional" Fear

Alice's mother may need to deal with false ideas and fears, that damage her relationship with her daughter.

a. Is there any basis for a parent to think that s/he can cleanse the past by pushing the child toward perfectionism? (1 John 4:11-13, 17-18)
_____

b. Can rules and domination alone prevent a child from becoming a parent too soon? (Zechariah 4:6)
_____

c. What is the best way for a parent to prepare a young person for life outside of the home? (Proverbs 22:6; Leviticus 26:3-4, 6-8)
_____

d. Does God give the primary responsibility for providing spiritual guidance for a child to the parents or the church? (Ephesians 6:4)
_____

e. What is the best attitude for Alice and her mother to have about her mother's young pregnancy? (2 Chronicles 7:14; Ezekiel 18:4, 19-24, 30-31)
_____

f. How can a counselor use the information presented in exercises a-e to help a parent who has beliefs that lead to dysfunctional fear?
_____

CASE STUDY ON FEAR

3. FEAR OF LOSS OF LOVE
Alice's mother has few friends of her own and seems to hesitate to become involved with the church that Alice attends. She also fears losing her relationship with her daughter to other people.
a. Will Alice's mother have someone to love her when Alice grows up? (John 14:18; Joshua 1:5; Ephesians 1:3-7)

b. How can the community of faith become family for both the mother and daughter? (Matthew 12:46-50; Ephesians 2:8-22; 1 Corinthians 12:13)

c. Does Alice's mother have a place set aside for her in the body of Christ? (1 Corinthians 12:12-18; Ephesians 2:6-10)

d. How can Alice's mother become a part of the community of faith? (Acts 16:31; 12:13; Hebrews 11:1-12:2)

e. Does God intend for the members of the community of faith to love and care for Alice's mother, a single parent? (Leviticus 19:18, 34; 1 John 4:8, 21; Romans 13:9)

f. How can a counselor use the information presented in exercises a-e to help a parent who fears losing her child's love?

4. DISTINGUISHING BETWEEN FEAR AND RESPECT
Alice's mother feels that Alice is disrespectful because she shared her real feelings without fear. She wanted to slap "the fear of God" into her.
a. Does "fear" in biblical terms mean being afraid of harm from God or anticipation of good from God? (Jeremiah 32:40-41)

b. Does a person accept Christ because fear of God or love from God? (1 John 4:18-19)

c. Do parents gain respect by beating it into children? (Ephesians 6:4)

d. Is it better to beat a child into submission or train a child? (Proverbs 22:6)

e. Should parents listen to a child or do all of the talking and make the child listen? (Ephesians 5:19-21; 6:4)

f. How can a counselor use the information from questions a-e to help a parent who feels that s/he gains respect from children by making them afraid and using excessive corporal punishment?

5. Trusting God and His People for Love and Protection

Alice's mother needs to learn how to trust God for love and for protection for herself and for her daughter.

a. What role will her mother's personal relationship with God have in protecting both mother and daughter? (Job 11:13-20)

b. What hidden lesson about parenting can be found in the story of Jesus' healing of Tabitha, the daughter of the ruler of the synagogue? (Mark 5:35-42)

c. What role does faith in God have in the parent/child relationship? (Hebrews 11:1-3, 32-35; Luke 7:11-15)

d. Does a parent need to keep a teenager in the house within eyesight in order for the teenager to be healed and/or protected by God? (John 5:46-54)

e. How does Scripture support the idea of single parents being a part of the community of faith along with their children? (Matthew 12:46-50)

f. How can a counselor use the information from questions a-e to guide a single parent into a closer relationship with God?

6. MINISTRY APPLICATION

Design a support group for parenting teenagers.

Focus Scripture: _____

Objectives:
a._____

b._____

1. Why is this ministry necessary?
a._____

b._____

2. List 10 topics for discussion.

a._____   f._____
b._____   g._____
c._____   h._____
d._____   i._____
e._____   j._____

3. What type of activities could the church host to encourage positive interaction between parents and teenagers?
a._____

b._____

c._____

4. How can the group measure its success?
a._____

b._____

c._____

7. PERSONAL APPLICATION

Describe occasions when fear has controlled your life.
___
___

What does 2 Timothy 1:7 mean to you?
___
___

How has fear hurt your relationship with God?
___
___

Is there hope? Explain. (1 John 4:18)
___
___

Does fear keep you from stepping out on faith and trusting God?
___
___

Speak 2 Timothy 1:7 to yourself every time you feel afraid.

CHAPTER EIGHT

CASE STUDY ON ABANDONMENT

INSTRUCTIONS: The following exercises apply principles presented in this chapter to a case study involving Cheryl, a person who feels abandoned. The Bible Application exercises consist of five "discovery" questions (a-e), followed by a summary question (f). The Ministry Application section provides an opportunity for participants to incorporate some of these precepts in their local churches. The Personal Application portion encourages self-examination on the subject of abandonment.

CHERYL

The Women's Fellowship at St. Luke's Presbyterian Church had been visiting the Lewis Home for Girls for more than a year now. During that time two women from the group had adopted children from the home. However, Mrs. Watkins was having trouble with Cheryl, the girl she had selected.

She had enrolled Cheryl in the church tutorial program, for help with mathematics, but the tutor had reported that Cheryl was withdrawn and sometimes cried if she was "pushed too hard." Mrs. Watkins told the president of the Women's Fellowship that Cheryl had a long history of serious problems.

Cheryl was only 11 years old when she came to the Lewis Home for Girls. Her records showed that she was above average in intelligence. However, she was depressed, having been separated from her five brothers and sisters, and having lost contact with her parents and other members of her parents' families.

Cheryl's parents had once been hardworking and responsible but had become addicted to cocaine. They had spent all of their money on drugs. Both lost their jobs. The father died of an overdose in Cheryl's presence. After that, the mother abandoned the children altogether. A truancy officer from the public schools had discovered the situation and reported it to the police. The children were taken from the mother and placed in various homes.

Cheryl came into contact with Mrs. Watkins through the outreach program of the Women's Fellowship. The Women's Fellowship regularly sponsored social activities for the girls at the Lewis Home and held Bible studies there. One day Cheryl's social worker told her that she had been selected to be Mrs. Watkins's adopted child. This is how Cheryl came to live at the Watkins home.

Mrs. Watkins decided to spend more time with Cheryl, encouraging the girl to talk about her problems and to determine whether Cheryl should be referred for professional help.

BIBLE APPLICATION EXERCISES

1. WHAT GOD THINKS OF CHILDREN

Children who have been abandoned are often uncertain about whether they have a right to be a child. Many have been forced into adult roles before they were ready. Many are unsure whether they should feel guilty for not being able to handle adult roles.

a. In what manner did the Lord come to earth? (Isaiah 9:6; 11:6; Luke 2:10-14) What does this indicate God thinks about children?_____

_____

b. What is evidence that the Lord loves children? (Matthew 11:1-6; 19:13-16)_____

_____

God's Power to Help Hurting People

c. What are some ways that the Lord expressed His love for children? (Matthew 15:21-28; Luke 7:1-15; John 4:46-54) _____
_____

d. Who are some of the children of the Bible that the Lord loved? (Exodus 1:15-16; 2:1-10; Matthew 9:18-26; Mark 9:17-27)
_____

e. How has the Lord expressed His love for specific children like Cheryl? (Psalm 139)
_____

f. Considering your answers to questions a-e, how should a foster parent, adoptive parent, or lay counselor help an abandoned child feel that it is all right to be a child?
_____

2. God's Family

Abandoned children are often confused about their relationships with parents. They may feel that they are responsible for their parents and that it is wrong for them to expect their parents to take care of them. What does God expect from parents?

a. Proverbs 22:6 _____
_____

b. Ephesians 6:4 _____
_____

c. Every believer is a part of whose family? (Ephesians 1:1-14) _____

d. What type of father is God? (1 John 3:1-3) _____

e. What type of mother is God? (Isaiah 66:13-14) _____

f. Considering your answers to questions a-e, how should a foster parent, adoptive parent or lay counselor help an abandoned child to acquire a realistic idea about a child's relationship with his/her parents?
_____
_____

3. The Presence of God

Abandoned children need to know that, if they turn their lives over to Christ, they will never be alone. What do the following Scriptures say about the presence of God?

a. Psalm 27:10 _____

CASE STUDY ON ABANDONMENT

b. Psalm 37:25 _____

c. Psalm 23 _____

d. 2 Corinthians 4:7-9 _____

e. Psalm 16:11; 140:13 _____

f. How can the foster parent, adoptive parent, or lay counselor use the previous Scriptures to lead an abandoned child into an intimate relationship with the Lord?
_____

4. A New Self-Image

God provides the basis of a new self-image for the abandoned child. What makes up the foundation of a child's self-image?

a. Proverbs 20:11 _____

b. Exodus 19:5-6; 1 Peter 2:5, 9 _____

c. Psalm 139:13-17 _____

d. Genesis 1:27 _____

e. 1 Corinthians 12 _____

f. How can the foster parent, adoptive parent, or lay counselor use the previous Scriptures to help an abandoned child develop a better self-image?
_____
_____

5. Learning New Skills

The Lord provides the basis for the abandoned child to develop new skills to cope with life. What are the fundamental ways in which a child can be prepared for a successful adult life?

a. Psalm 16:8-11 _____

b. Psalm 119:11 _____

c. 2 Timothy 2:15 _____

d. Hebrews 10:25 _____

e. Matthew 25:14-30 _____

f. How can the foster parent, adoptive parent, or lay counselor use the previous Scriptures to help an abandoned child prepare for a successful adult life?
_____
_____

6. MINISTRY APPLICATION

Design a volunteer partnership program between your church and a local foster care agency.

Focus Scripture: _____

Objectives:

a._____

b._____

1. List five topics for workshops.

a._____   d._____

b._____   e._____

c._____

2. Select one holiday and then describe how the church can use it to create a special event for abandoned children.

a._____

b._____

3. List five subject areas in which the church can sponsor tutorial programs for elementary age children.

a._____   d._____

b._____   e._____

c._____

4. Describe some strategies that the church could use to recruit tutors.

a._____
b._____
c._____

5. What are some ways that the church could sponsor job/college training for high school students?

a._____
b._____
c._____

7. PERSONAL APPLICATION

Describe a time when you have felt abandoned.
_____
_____
_____
_____

What does Hebrews 13:5 mean to you?
_____
_____
_____
_____
_____

How does the idea of Jesus Christ as Emmanuel relate to your situation?
_____
_____
_____
_____
_____

Take time today to pray for God's direction to encourage a child who struggles with abandonment issues. (Proverbs 11:25)

CHAPTER NINE

CASE STUDY ON FRUSTRATION

INSTRUCTIONS: The following exercises apply principles presented in this chapter to a case study involving Scott, a person who is hurting from frustration. The Bible Application exercises consist of five "discovery" questions (a-e), followed by a summary question (f). The Ministry Application section provides an opportunity for participants to incorporate some of these ideas in their local church. The Personal Application portion encourages self-examination on the subject of frustration.

SCOTT

Brother Daniels was driving along Payne Street near his church when he noticed Scott standing on the corner with some other young men. All of them seemed to be aimlessly staring into space. Brother Daniels pulled over to the curb, rolled his window down, and called Scott to the car. He hadn't seen Scott for over a year, and he wondered why the young man had stopped coming to youth meetings.

When Scott came over to the car, Brother Daniels opened the door and invited him to get in so that they could talk. It was then that Scott told him what had happened to him. Scott had just been released from jail a few months ago, where he had spent six months. Scott was very depressed, because he had spent time in jail for something that he hadn't done.

Apparently he was working at a sales job in a department store when the incident that led to his jail sentence took place. On that day, his cousin, who was visiting him from out of town, pushed Scott into a woman who was standing near his work area. The woman thought she was being attacked, so she started defending herself. Scott was arrested, and his cousin ran away, refusing to come to Scott's defense. By the time of his trial, Scott's cousin had left town.

Since Scott had been out of jail, he had been unable to find a job. He didn't have any money, and spent most of his time "hanging out" with friends on the corner. He was beginning to feel like a bum. He had worked very hard to finish high school and at one time had aspirations to go to college. One of the things he never wanted to happen was to have a prison record.

Recently, he had tried to enroll in school at a local college, but he could not locate any scholarships or a job that would pay the expenses. He mentioned that he was becoming desperate. Several of his friends had decided to sell or deliver drugs in order to "make ends meet." As a Christian, he really didn't want to get involved with this, but he didn't know how long he could hold out.

BIBLE APPLICATION EXERCISES

1. HOLDING ON

The frustrated person should not abandon his/her Christian principles but use them to solve the problems causing the frustration. What are two reasons for holding on to one's faith in spite of present difficulties?

a. Philippians 1:27-28 _____

b. Hebrews 3:12-13 _____

CASE STUDY ON FRUSTRATION

c. How does one know that Jesus understands the frustration of being tempted to turn away from a godly lifestyle? (Hebrews 4:14-15; Matthew 26:36-39) _____
_____

d. Will everyone's behavior remain consistent with Christian beliefs in spite of persecution? (1 Timothy 4:1-2) _____

e. As a community of believers, how can we help one another to hold on to our faith in spite of difficulties? (Hebrews 10:23-39; 11:1-3) _____
_____

f. How can the information from questions a-e be used to help frustrated people, such as Scott from the case study?
_____
_____

2. Faith

One of the cures for frustration is looking beyond current circumstances and exercising faith in God. Describe each person who exercised faith and obeyed God in spite of frustrating circumstances.

a. Hebrews 11:7; Genesis 6:1-9; 9:1-17 _____

b. Luke 1:1-24 _____

c. Hebrews 11:35; Luke 13:11-13 _____

d. John 21:1-14 _____

e. What is faith? What is the basis of it? (Hebrews 11:1-3; 12:1-4)
_____

f. How can the information from questions a-e be used to help frustrated people, such as Scott from the case study?
_____
_____

3. Appreciating Oneself

Often circumstances of this world send out messages to African Americans that are different from the messages that God sends.

a. What does God think of God's people? (Ephesians 1:3-10) _____
_____

b. What evidence is there, in the Word of God, that each person God created is a work of art? (Psalm 139:14-17) _____

c. What evidence is there that African Americans have just as much potential as other people? (12:1-14)
_____
_____
_____

d. Are difficult things always due to a person being bad? (Job 1:1-22) _____

e. What evidence is there that God will not allow God's people to perish? (John 3:16; Luke 15:11-32)
_____
_____
_____

f. How can the information from questions a-e be used to help frustrated people, such as Scott from the case study?
_____
_____
_____

4. REJOICING IN THE MIDST OF DIFFICULTIES

a. What is the proper response to have when we become frustrated by injustice? (Ephesians 4:26-28)
_____
_____
_____

b. What evidence is there that God does not intend for God's people to remain in oppressive and frustrating circumstances? (Luke 4:16-21) _____
_____

c. What evidence is there that God will deliver those who are frustrated by financial problems? (Luke 12:22-32) _____
_____
_____

d. Why should the Christian rejoice in the midst of difficulties? (Hebrews 12:1-3; Romans 8:29)
_____
_____
_____

CASE STUDY ON FRUSTRATION

f. How can the information from questions a-e be used to help frustrated people, such as Scott from the case study?
___
___

5. Locating Alternative Goals

God often has goals for us that are different from the goals we have for ourselves. Describe how God's goals were different from each person's goal for themselves.

a. Paul (Acts 8:3; 9: 3-9; 22:4; 26:11)___
___
___

b. John (Mark 1:20; 3:17; John 1:35-43; 19:26, 27; Revelation 22:20)
___
___
___

c. Peter (Matthew 4:18-22; Mark 1:16; Luke 5:10)___

d. Matthew (Matthew 9:9-10; Mark 2:14-15; Luke 5:27-29)___

e. Mary Magdalene (Luke 8:2; 23:49; Mark 16:1, 19; John 20:11-18)
___
___
___

f. How can the information from questions a-e be used to help frustrated people, such as Scott from the case study?
___
___
___

6. MINISTRY APPLICATION

Develop a "Discover Your Gifts" seminar.

Focus Scripture:
_____

Objectives:
a._____
b._____

Motivational Speakers:
_____
_____

Build some workshops around spiritual gifts.

Gift	Possible Careers
Apostles	_____
Prophets	_____
Teachers	_____
Power (administration)	_____
Healing	_____
Forms of Assistance	_____
Kinds of Tongues	_____

CASE STUDY ON FRUSTRATION

7. PERSONAL APPLICATION

What situations frustrate you?
___
___

What does Job 42:2 mean to you?
___
___

What role does the Holy Spirit play? (John 16:13)
___
___

Journalize frustrations as they occur, during the day and night, then pray for God's wisdom and direction in dealing with them.
___
___
___
___
___
___
___
___
___
___

CHAPTER TEN

CASE STUDY ON DEPRESSION

INSTRUCTIONS: The following exercises involve applying principles from this chapter to a case study and developing guidelines for establishing a counseling ministry in a local church. Lay counselors who service depressed people can use these guidelines. The Bible Application exercises consist of five "discovery" questions (a-e), followed by a summary question (f). The Ministry Application section provides an opportunity for participants to incorporate some of these ideas in their local church. The Personal Application portion encourages self-examination of each participant on the subject of depression.

MRS. HAMILTON

It was Mrs. Hamilton's first counseling session with Mrs. Fleming of the Counseling Ministry at Beacon Street Baptist Church. Mrs. Fleming noticed that this first meeting was very difficult for Mrs. Hamilton. She was extremely nervous and wept frequently. Once Mrs. Fleming was able to calm her down, she began describing very difficult and painful experiences.

For the past two years, she had been living with Bill, her live-in lover. She had met him through a friend. Bill had been kind to her five children as well as to her before he lost his job. Then his behavior changed. She soon learned that Bill had never kept a job for more than two years. According to his sister, he had always been irresponsible. His sister had thought that he was so attracted to this new family that he might become more stable, but he had not.

It wasn't long after Bill lost his job that his behavior changed. Bill expressed resentment over Mrs. Hamilton's attending church as frequently as she had begun to do, and he began questioning her as to whether she was really going to church. Although she urged him to come to church with her, he refused. Therefore she had started attending church less frequently, and had become very depressed.

She said that her relationship with this man was almost as bad as the one she had with her former husband. She had always been a great conversationalist and had many friends. However, her former husband had also become jealous of her friendships outside of the home. She talked about how much her relationship with her ex-husband depressed her.

Considering the fact that this was her second major relationship with a man, and it was almost as bad as her relationship with her former husband, she had low self-esteem. She spent most of her time wondering what was wrong with her. She had set a goal of having a marriage that was as happy as that of her maternal grandparents. She had even tried to select men who were similar to her grandfather, and had asked the men to do things she had observed her grandmother asking her grandfather to do. She could not understand why she had "failed" in two relationships.

BIBLE APPLICATION EXERCISES

1. UNDERSTANDING

Jesus understood the woman who was about to be stoned for adultery (John 8:1-11). What were two ways in which Jesus showed he understood the woman caught in adultery?

a. John 8:7-9 _____

b. John 8:9-11 _____

c. What were the attitudes of the Pharisees and others toward people with problems? (Luke 15:21; 18:11-12) _____

CASE STUDY ON DEPRESSION

d. Usually, how were "harlots" treated? (Genesis 38:24-25; Leviticus 21:9)
_____

e. How does the Mosaic Law handle adultery? (Leviticus 20:10) How did the accusers interpret the law differently? (John 8:4-5)
_____

f. How can the story of Jesus' treatment of the woman caught in adultery serve as a model for counselors dealing with depressed people?
_____

2. BEING PATIENT

Jesus patiently counseled His disciples and the sisters of Lazarus, even though their immature grasp of spiritual truth grieved Him (John 11:1-46). How does one know that certain people around Jesus did not fully understand who He was or the truths He presented?

a. His disciples (John 11:7-13, 16) _____

   What was Jesus' reaction? (11:14-17) _____

b. Mary (John 11:20-24) _____

   What was Jesus' reaction? (11:25-26) _____

c. Martha (John 11:32-33) _____

   What was Jesus' reaction? (11:33-34) _____

d. Jewish people (John 11:37) _____

   What was Jesus' reaction? (11:38-43) _____

e. What was the outcome of Jesus' patience and persistence with the spiritually immature people surrounding Him? (John 11:44-46)_____

f. How did Jesus help the woman at the well to clarify her problem? What techniques did He use? What traits did He exhibit? How can this story be used as a model for helping counselees clarify problems?
_____
_____

3. CLARIFYING THE PROBLEM

The story of the woman of Samaria at the well illustrates how Jesus helped a counselee to clarify a problem. What were two sources of the woman's confusion?

a. John 4:11, 13-15 _____

b. John 4:10, 12 _____

God's Power to Help Hurting People

c. What was the woman's basic problem? (4:16-24) _____

d. What relationship existed between the Jews and the Samaritans? (John 4:9) _____

e. What was the outcome of Jesus' counseling session with the woman at the well? (4:28-30) _____

f. How did Jesus help the woman at the well to clarify her problem? What techniques did He use? What traits did He exhibit? How can this story be used as a model for helping counselees clarify problems?
_____
_____

4. ALLOWING THE COUNSELEE TO SHOW EMOTION

Jesus didn't condemn a weeping woman He met for expressing her emotions (Luke 7:36-50).

a. Describe the expressed emotions of the woman who fell at Jesus' feet. (1 Samuel 25:23-24; 2 Kings 4:36-37; Esther 8:3) _____

b. Describe the expressed emotions of the woman who kissed Jesus' feet. (Isaiah 49:22-3; 1 Kings 19:18) _____

c. Why was this woman so upset about being considered a sinner? (Luke 7:37; 15:21; 18:11-12; Genesis 38:24-25; Leviticus 21:9) _____

d. What did Jesus see beneath the woman's emotions? What was Jesus' reaction to her? (Luke 7:40-50) _____

e. What was the outcome of Jesus allowing this counselee to express emotion? (Luke 7:49-50) _____

f. How can the story of the weeping woman be used as a model for those who counsel depressed persons?
_____

5. THE LORD'S HELP

The Lord has resources for the depressed. Examine each of the following Scriptures, and identify the promises that the Lord makes to the depressed person.

a. John 8:12 _____
b. John 4:13-14 _____
c. Matthew 21:22 _____
d. Luke 11:9-13 _____
e. James 1:17; John 14:15-21 _____

f. What hope do the above Scriptures provide for the counselor and counselee?
_____

6. MINISTRY APPLICATION

Develop strategies for encouraging and engaging depressed believers.

Focus Scripture: _____

Objectives:
a. _____
b. _____

Instructions: Select an example of a depressed person from the section of the chapter, "Develop Strategies and Identify Resources." Write out a plan to help this person.

Person:
_____

Plan:
_____
_____
_____
_____
_____
_____
_____
_____
_____
_____
_____
_____
_____
_____

7. PERSONAL APPLICATION

Are you or have you ever felt depressed?
_____
_____
_____

What is causing you to feel depressed?
_____
_____
_____

What does Psalm 42 mean to you?
_____
_____
_____

Do you know of a trusted friend who can help you?
_____
_____
_____

Which Psalms of Praise can help with your healing? How?
_____
_____
_____

Study Psalms of Praise as one step toward healing.

CHAPTER ELEVEN

CASE STUDY ON ANGER

INSTRUCTIONS: In the following story, Robert is experiencing anger that is in part due to conflicts within his family. The following exercises will lead to an in-depth study of Robert's problem and will provide the opportunity to apply principles covered in this chapter to helping people with similar problems.

The Bible Application exercises consist of five "discovery" questions (a-e), followed by a summary question (f). The Ministry Application section provides an opportunity for participants to incorporate some of these precepts in their local church. The Personal Application portion encourages self-examination on the subject of anger.

ROBERT

Brother Boyd of Bible Community Baptist Church and head of the prison ministry, took his small group of volunteers to the city jail. When Brother Boyd entered the chapel, he was met by a young man who was waiting for him and seemed to know who he was. At first Brother Boyd didn't recognize the young man. Then, as the young man told his story, Brother Boyd remembered.

Brother Boyd hadn't seen Robert since he was eleven years old. He had caught Brother Boyd's attention when, with a cigarette in his mouth and a knife in his hand, he had terrorized the staff at the church youth drop-in center. At that time, he had threatened to blow up the entire church.

Today, at 19 years of age, the toughness that was once considered "cute" by the church staff had turned hard. However, Brother Boyd could see beneath the hardness to the tears that surfaced in Robert's eyes as he told Brother Boyd his story. Robert told Brother Boyd that he had watched as his father shot one of his brothers on their front porch. After that, all of his brothers had been in trouble with the police. He was the third one to be incarcerated. One brother had already been deported to Jamaica, his family's native country.

Robert went on to describe a family situation that was disorganized. He had grown up listening to his father and mother arguing over whether they should both become American citizens. Their mother really didn't seem to want to remain in this country. The brothers had learned to "play off" the mother against the father to get what they wanted. The mother would often lie for them, so that they could get their way.

Robert was in jail because he had broken into a neighborhood store and had been arrested. He was convicted of armed robbery.

BIBLE APPLICATION EXERCISES

1. SELF-DISCOVERY

It is important for young people who are angry to discover the potential they have in God, in spite of failures they may have experienced. It is also important for them to discover how important they are to God.

a. In whose image is everyone created? (Genesis 1:27, 31; 2:7)

_____

b. What does God think of the human beings God created? (Psalm 139:13-17)

_____

God's Power to Help Hurting People

c. How important are young people to God? (Romans 8:39; Psalm 139:1-12)

d. What is the highest potential that a young person can have? (Exodus 19:6; 1 Peter 2:9)

e. What does God think of young people? (Mark 9:35-7; Matthew 18:3-6; 19:13-14)

f. How can the information from questions a-e be used to help young people, like Robert from the case study, who are angry and confused?

2. Structure

Many angry young people come from chaotic backgrounds. It is important for young people to experience the benefits of structure when they come from disorganized backgrounds. Describe the biblical accounts that illustrate the power of a program that is organized under God's direction.

a. Genesis 6:13-7:1; 7:18-21; 8:14-16 _____

b. Joshua 6:1-4, 15-21 _____

c. Judges 7:2-7, 19-21 _____

d. What evidence is there that order and structure are important to God? (Genesis 1:1-10; 1 Corinthians 14:33) _____

e. What are the arguments in favor of organized programs? (1 Corinthians 14:40; Ecclesiastes 12:9-10)

f. How can the information from questions a-e form the rationale for organizing programs to help young people, such as Robert from the case study?

3. Meaningful Relationships

Angry young people need to know that they, too, can have meaningful relationships with adults. However, many adults mistakenly believe that all young people should be "seen and not heard." Use the scriptural references below to describe the positive interactions between adults and young people.

CASE STUDY ON ANGER

a. 1 Samuel 1:11, 24-28; 2:11, 18, 19; 3:3-4, 16-20 _____

b. Luke 2:22-41 _____

c. Luke 7:11-15 _____

d. John 2:1-11 _____

e. Matthew 15:21-28; Mark 7:24-30 _____

f. Based on the information from questions a-e, what are the arguments against young people merely being seen by adults and not heard?
_____
_____
_____

4. Values

Angry young people who come out of a disorganized environment may need to adopt a new set of values in order to have success in life.

a. How should accepting Christ change the way a young person views the world? (Romans 12:12)
_____
_____

b. What is the scriptural basis for seeing life differently than people in the world see it? (1 John 2:15)
_____
_____

c. What is the ultimate goal of the Christian? (1 Corinthians 13:12) What does this mean for the young person? _____
_____

d. When a young person's values change, does this mean that s/he is allowed to show disrespect toward his/her parents? (Exodus 20:12; Deuteronomy 5:16; Matthew 15:4; 19:19; Ephesians 6:1-3)
_____
_____
_____

e. Who becomes the young person's guide when they make a decision to follow Christ? (Psalm 16:11; 23)
_____
_____
_____

f. How could the information above help young people, such as Robert, to adopt new values for their lives?
_____
_____

5. Making Decisions

Critical decisions must be made when dealing with the sources of anger and frustration. Young people as well as adults must make these decisions.

a. What is the most fundamental choice that any human being must make? (Joshua 24:15; John 14:6)
___

b. Why is it so important for young people to be willing to make decisions? (Matthew 7:14; James 1:6-8)
___

c. Is it enough to make an initial decision to follow Christ? (1 Timothy 6:12; 1 Corinthians 16:13; Ephesians 6: 10-18)
___

d. How does a young person learn to make correct decisions? (Psalm 48:14; Jeremiah 3:4; Psalm 31:3)
___

e. How could an adult lead young people to make correct decisions? (Deuteronomy 4:7-9; Proverbs 22:6; Titus 2:1-8; Ephesians 6:4)
___
___
___

f. How can the information from questions a-e be used to help young people such as Robert learn to make correct decisions?
___
___
___

CASE STUDY ON ANGER

6. MINISTRY APPLICATION

Develop a ministry for incarcerated young people.

Focus Scripture:
_____

Objectives:
a._____
b._____

1. List the type of training necessary for church laity.

   a._____
   b._____
   c._____

2. Develop the list of resources that the church could provide for these volunteers.

   a. Transportation
   _____

   b. Communication
   _____

   c. Literature
   _____

   d. Counseling
   _____

3. List ways in which the church could assist newly released convicts.

   a._____
   b._____
   c._____

4. What obstacles may the church have to overcome in order to be effective in this ministry?

   a._____
   b._____
   c._____

7. PERSONAL APPLICATION

What situations cause you to experience anger?
_____
_____

How do you express your anger? (Ephesians 4:26)
_____
_____
_____

Does it fit in the realm of godly anger? (Matthew 21:13)
_____
_____
_____

What are some ways that you could manage anger? (2 Peter 1:6)
_____
_____
_____

Confide, in a trusted friend, your struggles with anger for accountability and begin to write out godly ways of expressing anger.

CHAPTER TWELVE

CASE STUDY ON LONELINESS

INSTRUCTIONS: In the following story, Mrs. Simpson is experiencing painful loneliness. The following exercises will lead you into an in-depth study of Mrs. Simpson's problem, and an opportunity to apply principles from the chapter to it.

The Bible Application exercises consist of five "discovery" questions (a-e), followed by a summary question (f). The Ministry Application section provides an opportunity for participants to incorporate some of these precepts in their local church. The Personal Application portion encourages self-examination for each participant on the subject of loneliness.

MRS. SIMPSON

It was Tuesday night and Deacon Green was doing sick visitation in the senior citizens' complex, where many members of Beacon Street A.M.E. lived. When he reached 80-year-old Mrs. Belle Simpson's home, he knocked on the door, but no one answered. This seemed unusual, so Deacon Green rang the bell of Mrs. Adams, the floor captain on Mrs. Simpson's floor. Mrs. Adams came out and said that she had seen Mrs. Simpson earlier, and she believed that Mrs. Simpson was still in her apartment. Mrs. Adams rushed back into her apartment and phoned security.

Mr. Bryant, the security guard, rushed over and opened the door. When the door was opened, Mrs. Simpson could be seen sitting by her window, staring into space. When they tried to talk to her, she was unresponsive.

Mr. Bryant immediately called an ambulance, and Mrs. Simpson was rushed to the nearby hospital. In the days that followed, Mrs. Simpson's son, who flew in from Mississippi, notified Deacon Green that Mrs. Simpson was successfully treated at the hospital, but had been suffering from a mild stroke and was in an acute state of malnutrition.

Raymond Simpson informed Deacon Green that his mother had been widowed 12 years ago, and for the past 10 years had been living alone in the senior's complex. During that time period, a number of her close friends had gone on to be with the Lord. Because she had stopped driving, she couldn't regularly attend church or be at meetings of the senior club at the church. She didn't want to be a bother to others.

Raymond informed Deacon Green that Mrs. Adams, the floor captain, had told him that Mrs. Simpson had recently said she had lost her appetite. She had stopped cooking, saying that it was too much trouble to cook and eat alone. Most of her meals consisted of cereal and milk. Her only company, for days at a time, was the television. The telephone rarely rang.

BIBLE APPLICATION EXERCISES

1. THE ROLE OF THE CHURCH

Mrs. Simpson had lost contact with her family and church.

a. Should Mrs. Simpson continue to stay at home instead of attending worship services at her church? (Hebrews 10:25) _____

b. Does the church have a responsibility for transporting such people as Mrs. Simpson to ministry activities? (Acts 6:1-7; 1 Corinthians 12:23-26; Matthew 25:34-40) _____

God's Power to Help Hurting People

c. Does Mrs. Simpson's family have a responsibility for meeting her needs? (Exodus 20:12; Ephesians 6:2) _____

d. Can an elderly woman contribute to the community of faith? (1 Corinthians 7:7; 12:4-26) _____

e. What gift could the mature in Christ offer to the community of faith? (Hebrews 5:14) _____

f. Based on information from questions a-e, summarize the biblical foundation for churches and families helping people such as Mrs. Simpson combat painful loneliness. _____

2. A Relationship with Christ

It is difficult to deal with painful loneliness without a relationship with Jesus Christ.

a. Is Mrs. Simpson's church membership the same as a personal commitment to Christ (i.e., is born again)? (John 10:1) _____

b. Can Mrs. Simpson be "born again" as an elderly woman? (John 3:3-5, 16) _____

c. Does working in church most of one's life take the place of being born again? (Ephesians 2:9) _____

d. If Mrs. Simpson is not saved, what does she need to do in order to be born again? (John 3:16; Romans 10:9, 10) _____

e. How can salvation help Mrs. Simpson cope with loneliness? (John 15:4, 5; Hebrews 13:5; 1 Kings 19:11-12) _____

f. How can a counselor, deacon, or friend use the information in a-e to lead Mrs. Simpson to Christ, if she is not already a Christian? _____

3. Helping Others

One way of eliminating painful loneliness is by learning to help others. Mrs. Simpson may have gifts or skills that can be used to help others in the community of faith.

a. What is the gift of wisdom? List a specific way that an elderly woman with this gift might contribute to the community of faith. (1 Corinthians 2:6-12; 12:8) _____

b. What is the gift of faith? (1 Corinthians 12:9; Matthew 17:18-21) List a specific way that an elderly woman with this gift might contribute to the community of faith. _____

c. List three other gifts that an elderly person could contribute to the community of faith. (1 Corinthians 12) _____

CASE STUDY ON LONELINESS

d. Is Black history important? (Deuteronomy 6:10-19; Judges 2:11-19) List a specific way that an elderly African American woman could contribute to a community of faith in the area of Black history.
___

e. What role could an older woman have in the lives of younger women? (Titus 2:4)
___

f. Based on the answers to a-e, what are some ways that Mrs. Simpson can be encouraged to use her gifts to help others? What impact might these activities have on her painful experience of loneliness?
___

4. Using Time Productively

Self-help activities can be done which can counter the effects of loneliness. What activities could Mrs. Simpson do by herself to use the time productively?

a. 2 Timothy 2:15
___

What materials does she need?
___
___
___

b. Luke 2:36-37
___

c. Matthew 25:36
___

What equipment might she need to do this? What supplies? ___

d. What kind of goal could Mrs. Simpson strive to keep for her mind? (Philippians 2:4-5)
___
___
___

e. What goal could Mrs. Simpson do on a daily basis to keep from falling away from God? (Hebrews 3:13)___

f. How can a deacon, friend, or counselor use the information in a-e to help Mrs. Simpson learn to productively use the time that she spends alone?
___
___
___

5. BEING GRATEFUL!

Since Mrs. Simpson has been blessed with a long life, what are some of the things she can be thankful for?

a. Matthew 9:35

b. Philippians 4:13

c. Philippians 1:3-6

d. Psalm 23

e. John 14:16, 26; 15:26

f. How can a counselor, friend, deacon, or minister use the information from questions a-e to comfort Mrs. Simpson?

6. MINISTRY APPLICATION

Create a strategic plan for developing strong relationships in the bodies of believers.

Focus Scripture:
_____
_____
_____

Objectives:
a._____
b._____

1. What are some major obstacles to unity within the church?
a._____
b._____
c._____

2. How can a strong, united church eradicate loneliness within the body?
a._____
b._____
c._____

3. What kinds of activities could bridge the gap between different:

a. Age groups
_____

b. Racial backgrounds
_____

c. Socioeconomic classes
_____

7. PERSONAL APPLICATION

At what times do you feel lonely?
_____
_____

What steps could you take to reduce lonely feelings? (Proverbs 18:24)
_____
_____

In your life, how does Jesus relate to feelings of loneliness? (Matthew 26:37-44)
_____
_____

Why is loneliness a false feeling? (James 4:8)
_____
_____

Make a decision to get involved in volunteer activities in your church and community.

NOTES

NOTES

NOTES

NOTES

NOTES

NOTES